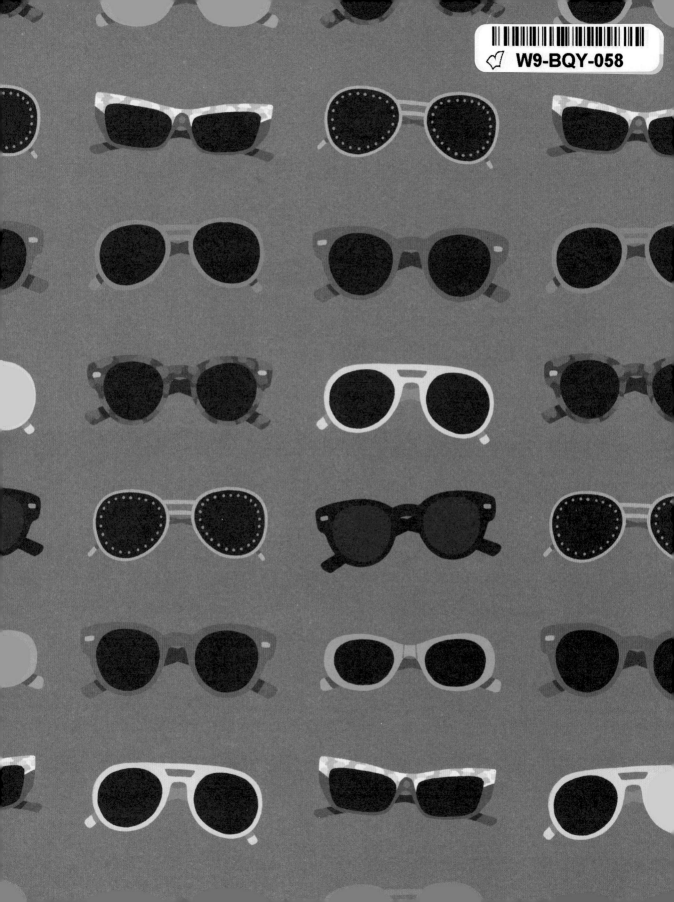

Little People, BIG DREAMS™
STEVIE WONDER

Written by
Maria Isabel Sánchez Vegara

Illustrated by
Melissa Lee Johnson

Frances Lincoln
Children's Books

One spring, a little child with a shiny smile was born in Michigan. His name was Stevie and he became blind a few days after he was born. He wouldn't grow to see the beautiful world around him, but he would feel it and hear it.

His family moved to Detroit and Stevie had to stay home a lot. To help pass the time, he began banging on pots and pans. Soon, he was playing his uncle's harmonica and a neighbor's old piano.

When Stevie heard people playing music in the street, he stopped and introduced himself. Clicking his fingers, he joined the party with a joyful voice, while John played the bongos.

He was just 11 years old when he signed his first music contract with Motown, a label working with his favorite African-American artists. Everyone was so amazed by his talent that they named him "Little Stevie Wonder."

As a member of the Motown Revue Tour, Stevie crossed the country in a ramshackle bus, composing songs on the road. He was always the first to go on stage and went to bed straight after his performance.

MUSI

He became the youngest artist ever to top the charts with a tune called "Fingertips." Stevie also wrote countless songs about love, peace, and all the things that are worth having in the world. They were full of groove and fun melodies.

For years, he had a tutor named Ted who wisely guided him. Ted also had limited eyesight, and loved music as much as Stevie did. He wrote a few songs, too. One of them ended up being a hit on one of Stevie's albums.

When Stevie's first daughter, Aisha, was born, he celebrated it with "Isn't She Lovely?", a song made with the pure love of a happy father. You can even hear Stevie bathing his daughter in its closing moments.

One day, Stevie was badly hurt in a car accident.
He fell asleep for four long days, and only woke up when
his good friend Ira was visiting. When Ira started singing
a gospel song, Stevie began to tap his fingers to the beat!

Stevie was committed to his community. To support those who wanted the birthday of Martin Luther King Junior to become a national holiday, he created a song. It was so full of joy that people still celebrate birthdays by singing it!

From rhythm & blues to soul, from funk to pop...
Stevie played everything! He even made the music
for a movie and won an Oscar for it. He first recorded
"I Just Called to Say I Love You" over the telephone!

ME

H LIEBE DICH

MAHAL KITA

사랑해

我爱你

TE QUIERO

With 25 Grammy Awards, he is one of the most celebrated artists of all time. Stevie was also named Messenger of Peace by the United Nations, and helped improve the lives of people with sensory, mental, and physical conditions.

And looking back at all the good friends and great songs he's made through the years, you can tell that Little Stevie isn't just an amazing musician, but a person whose joy can be felt by anyone who sings along with him.

STEVIE WONDER

(Born 1950)

1964

1974

Born Stevland Hardaway Judkins in Saginaw, Michigan, Stevie Wonder arrived six weeks earlier than his parents expected him. Doctors believe that too much oxygen at birth caused him to go blind when he was just a few days old. From an early age, Stevie's awareness of sound and a bright imagination helped him to create joyful, colorful music, teeming with positivity. As a young man in Detroit, he sang in his father's church choir and by the age of 9 he had learned to play the piano, drums and harmonica. During a performance for some of his friends, he was introduced to a producer at Motown Records, who signed Stevie immediately under the name "Little Stevie Wonder."

1980

2011

Aged 12, his hit single "Fingertips" was released on his album *The 12 Year Old Genius*, giving Motown its first ever chart-topping record. As well as performing, Stevie also began to write songs for other artists. Soon, he became known as a pioneer in music: a master of the electronic keyboard to rock musicians around the world; a voice of such range that he was the envy of jazz icons; and an activist whose words came straight from the heart and the gospel influences of his childhood. Creating catchy tunes with honesty and care that every person could sing along to, his music touched people's hearts and minds. Today he is one of the most successful musicians in history, recording ten US number-one hits and selling over 100 million records around the world.

Want to find out more about **Stevie Wonder?**

Have a read of these great books:

Who is Stevie Wonder? by Jim Gigliotti

Little Stevie Wonder by Quincy Troupe and Lisa Cohen

Brimming with creative inspiration, how-to projects, and useful information to enrich your everyday life, Quarto Knows is a favorite destination for those pursuing their interests and passions. Visit our site and dig deeper with our books into your area of interest: Quarto Creates, Quarto Cooks, Quarto Homes, Quarto Lives, Quarto Drives, Quarto Explores, Quarto Gifts, or Quarto Kids.

Published by Katie Cotton • Designed by Karissa Santos

Edited by Katy Flint and Rachel Williams • Production by Nikki Ingram

Editorial Assistance from Alex Hithersay

Manufactured In China CC112020

1 3 5 7 9 8 6 4 2

Photographic acknowledgements (pages 28-29, from left to right): 1. The American musician Stevie Wonder as a 14 year-old boy, with a harmonica, ca. 1964 © CBS/ullstein bild via Getty Images. 2. Photo of Stevie WONDER, 1974 © Photo by Ian Dickson/Redferns. 3. Stevie Wonder, portrait at The Grand Hotel Amsterdam, Netherlands, 1980, promoting the 'Hotter than July'album © Rico D'Rozario/Redferns. 4. Recording Artist Stevie Wonder performs onstage at 2011 MusiCares Person of the Year Tribute to Barbra Streisand at Los Angeles Convention Center on February 11, 2011 in Los Angeles, California. © Larry Busacca/WireImage.

Collect the Little People, BIG DREAMS™ series:

FRIDA KAHLO

ISBN: 978-1-84780-783-0

COCO CHANEL

ISBN: 978-1-84780-784-7

MAYA ANGELOU

ISBN: 978-1-84780-889-9

AMELIA EARHART

ISBN: 978-1-84780-888-2

AGATHA CHRISTIE

ISBN: 978-1-84780-960-5

MARIE CURIE

ISBN: 978-1-84780-962-9

ROSA PARKS

ISBN: 978-1-78603-018-4

AUDREY HEPBURN

ISBN: 978-1-78603-053-5

EMMELINE PANKHURST

ISBN: 978-1-78603-020-7

ELLA FITZGERALD

ISBN: 978-1-78603-087-0

ADA LOVELACE

ISBN: 978-1-78603-076-4

JANE AUSTEN

ISBN: 978-1-78603-120-4

GEORGIA O'KEEFFE

ISBN: 978-1-78603-122-8

HARRIET TUBMAN

ISBN: 978-1-78603-227-0

ANNE FRANK

ISBN: 978-1-78603-229-4

MOTHER TERESA

ISBN: 978-1-78603-230-0

JOSEPHINE BAKER

ISBN: 978-1-78603-228-7

L. M. MONTGOMERY

ISBN: 978-1-78603-233-1

JANE GOODALL

ISBN: 978-1-78603-231-7

SIMONE DE BEAUVOIR

ISBN: 978-1-78603-232-4

MUHAMMAD ALI

ISBN: 978-1-78603-331-4

STEPHEN HAWKING

ISBN: 978-1-78603-333-8

MARIA MONTESSORI

ISBN: 978-1-78603-755-8

VIVIENNE WESTWOOD

ISBN: 978-1-78603-757-2

MAHATMA GANDHI

ISBN: 978-1-78603-787-9

DAVID BOWIE

ISBN: 978-1-78603-332-1

WILMA RUDOLPH

ISBN: 978-1-78603-751-0

DOLLY PARTON

ISBN: 978-1-78603-760-2

BRUCE LEE

ISBN: 978-1-78603-789-3

RUDOLF NUREYEV

ISBN: 978-1-78603-791-6

ZAHA HADID

ISBN: 978-1-78603-745-9

MARY SHELLEY
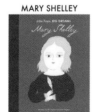
ISBN: 978-1-78603-748-0

MARTIN LUTHER KING JR.

ISBN: 978-0-7112-4567-9

DAVID ATTENBOROUGH

ISBN: 978-0-7112-4564-8

ASTRID LINDGREN

ISBN: 978-0-7112-5217-2

EVONNE GOOLAGONG

ISBN: 978-0-7112-4586-0

BOB DYLAN

ISBN: 978-0-7112-4675-1

ALAN TURING

ISBN: 978-0-7112-4678-2

BILLIE JEAN KING

ISBN: 978-0-7112-4693-5

GRETA THUNBERG

ISBN: 978-0-7112-5645-3

JESSE OWENS

ISBN: 978-0-7112-4583-9

JEAN-MICHEL BASQUIAT

ISBN: 978-0-7112-4580-8

ARETHA FRANKLIN

ISBN: 978-0-7112-4686-7

CORAZON AQUINO

ISBN: 978-0-7112-4684-3

PELÉ

ISBN: 978-0-7112-4573-0

ERNEST SHACKLETON

ISBN: 978-0-7112-4571-6

STEVE JOBS

ISBN: 978-0-7112-4577-8

AYRTON SENNA

ISBN: 978-0-7112-4672-0

LOUISE BOURGEOIS

ISBN: 978-0-7112-4690-4

ELTON JOHN

ISBN: 978-0-7112-5840-2

JOHN LENNON
ISBN: 978-0-7112-5767-2

PRINCE

ISBN: 978-0-7112-5439-8

CHARLES DARWIN

ISBN: 978-0-7112-5771-9

CAPTAIN TOM MOORE

ISBN: 978-0-7112-6209-6

HANS CHRISTIAN ANDERSEN

ISBN: 978-0-7112-5934-8

STEVIE WONDER

ISBN: 978-0-7112-5775-7

MEGAN RAPINOE

ISBN: 978-0-7112-5783-2

MARY ANNING

ISBN: 978-0-7112-5554-8

MALALA YOUSAFZAI
ISBN: 978-0-7112-5904-1

ACTIVITY BOOKS

STICKER ACTIVITY BOOK
ISBN: 978-0-7112-6012-2

COLORING BOOK
ISBN: 978-0-7112-6136-5

LITTLE ME, BIG DREAMS JOURNAL

ISBN: 978-0-7112-4889-2

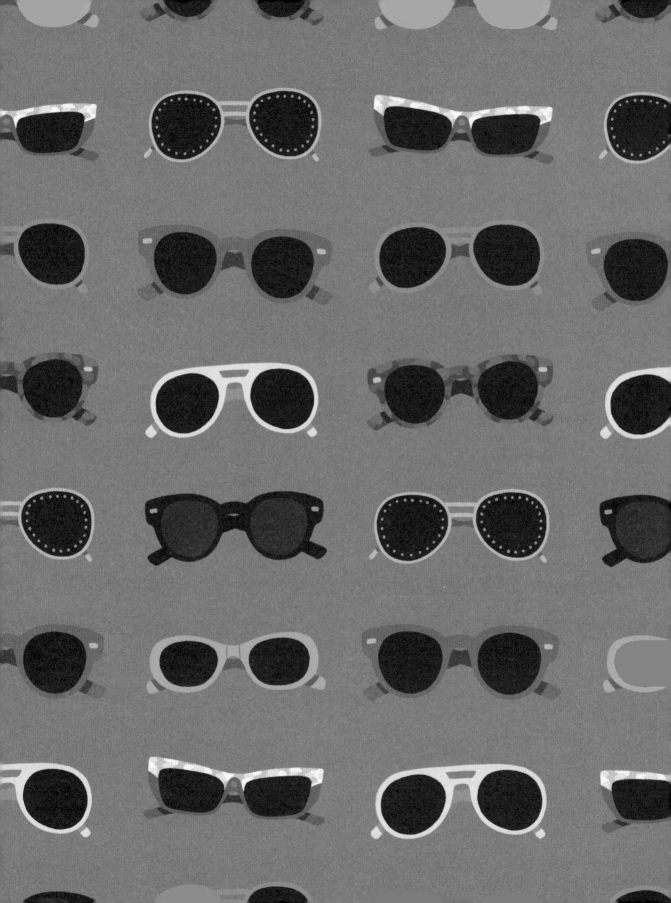